5-17

D0844575

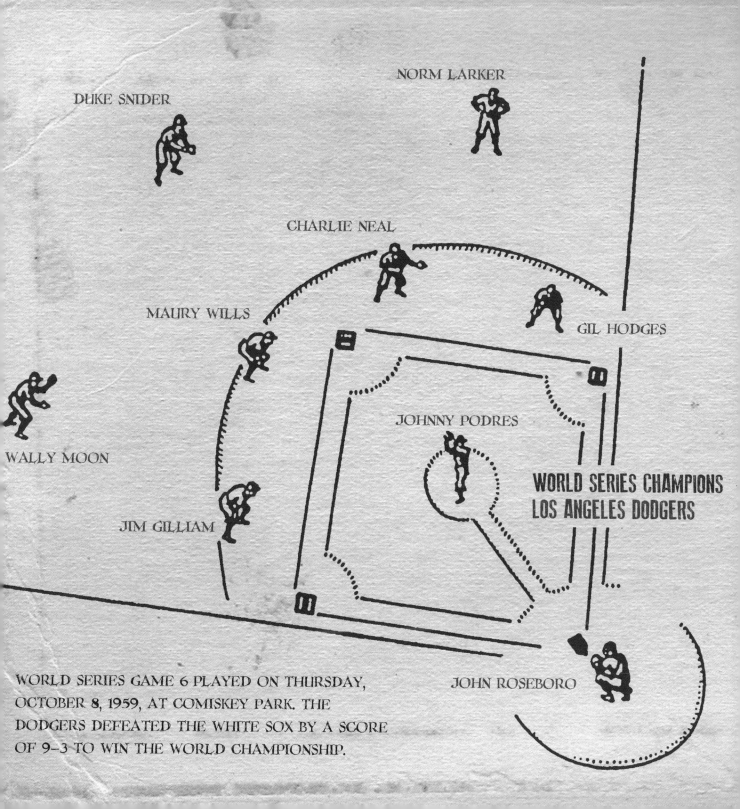

NORM LARKER

DUKE SNIDER

CHARLIE NEAL

MAURY WILLS

GIL HODGES

WALLY MOON

JOHNNY PODRES

WORLD SERIES CHAMPIONS
LOS ANGELES DODGERS

JIM GILLIAM

JOHN ROSEBORO

WORLD SERIES GAME 6 PLAYED ON THURSDAY,
OCTOBER 8, 1959, AT COMISKEY PARK. THE
DODGERS DEFEATED THE WHITE SOX BY A SCORE
OF 9-3 TO WIN THE WORLD CHAMPIONSHIP.

WORLD SERIES CHAMPIONS

LOS ANGELES DODGERS

SARA GILBERT

CREATIVE EDUCATION

Published by Creative Education
P.O. Box 227, Mankato, Minnesota 56002
Creative Education is an imprint of The Creative Company
www.thecreativecompany.us

Design and production by Blue Design (www.bluedes.com)
Art direction by Rita Marshall
Printed in the United States of America

Photographs by Corbis (Bettmann), Getty Images (Andrew D.
Bernstein, Lisa Blumenfeld, Diamond Images, John Dominis/
Time & Life Pictures, Stephen Dunn, Focus on Sport, Bob Gomel/
Time & Life Pictures, Jeff Gross, Scott Halleran/Allsport, Will Hart,
Eddie Hironaka, Ed Jackson/NY Daily News Archive, Kirby Lee/
WireImage, Ronald C. Modra, Ralph Morse/Time & Life Pictures,
National Baseball Hall of Fame Library/MLB Photos, Photo File/
MLB Photos, Louis Reqeuna/MLB Photos, Robert Riger, Mark
Rucker/Transcendental Graphics, Justin Sullivan)

Library of Congress Cataloging-in-Publication Data
Gilbert, Sara.
Los Angeles Dodgers / Sara Gilbert.
p. cm. — (World series champions)
Includes bibliographical references and index.
Summary: A simple introduction to the Los Angeles Dodgers major
league baseball team, including its start in 1884 in Brooklyn, its
World Series triumphs, and its stars throughout the years.
ISBN 978-1-60818-266-4
1. Los Angeles Dodgers (Baseball team)—History—Juvenile
literature. I. Title.
GV875.L6.G54 2013
796.357'640979494—dc23   2012004257

First edition
9 8 7 6 5 4 3 2 1

Cover: Center fielder Matt Kemp
Page 2: Pitcher Don Drysdale
Page 3: Pitcher Eric Gagne
Right: Dodgers players in 1942

TOMMY LASORDA

WILLIE DAVIS

FERNANDO VALENZUELA

ZACK WHEAT

KIRK GIBSON

ROY CAMPANELLA

TABLE OF CONTENTS

LOS ANGELES AND DODGER STADIUM

Los Angeles is a huge city in California. It is a sunny place with a lot of beaches. The sun also shines on a Los Angeles ballpark called Dodger Stadium. A baseball team called the Dodgers plays there.

LOS ANGELES AND DODGER STADIUM

RIVALS AND COLORS

The Dodgers are a major league baseball team. They play against other major-league teams to try to win the World Series and become world champions. The Dodgers wear blue and white uniforms. They play many games against their **RIVALS**, the San Francisco Giants.

PITCHER CHAD BILLINGSLEY

FIRST BASEMAN GIL HODGES

DODGERS HISTORY

The Dodgers played their first season in 1884 in Brooklyn, New York. They were called several different names then. When they got to the World Series in 1916 and 1920, they were called the Robins.

EBBETS FIELD IN BROOKLYN

JOHNNY PODRES

BRAD PENNY

MAURY WILLS

DAZZY VANCE

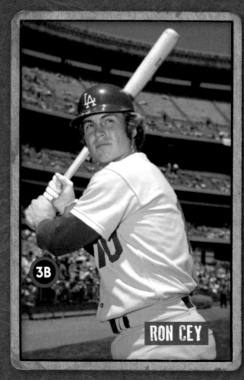

RON CEY

JOE McGINNITY

PEE WEE REESE

SECOND BASEMAN JACKIE ROBINSON

In the 1940s, shortstop Pee Wee Reese led the Dodgers to the
World Series three times. But they lost every time. Finally,
in 1955, the Dodgers beat the New York Yankees to become
world champions!

HIDEO NOMO

In 1958, the Dodgers moved to Los Angeles. They impressed their new fans by winning the World Series in 1959, 1963, and 1965. Manager Tommy Lasorda led the team to two more championships in 1981 and 1988.

The Dodgers were **CONTENDERS** after that, thanks to pitchers like Orel Hershiser and Hideo Nomo. They got to the **PLAYOFFS** many times. But they could not get back to the World Series.

OREL HERSHISER

JACKIE ROBINSON

SANDY KOUFAX

DODGERS STARS

In 1947, the Dodgers signed second baseman Jackie Robinson. He was the first black player in major-league history and became a big star for the Dodgers. Sandy Koufax was one of the best pitchers in baseball. He used a great curveball to win 165 games.

In 1981, Dodgers fans had fun watching pitcher Fernando Valenzuela throw **SCREWBALLS**. In 1992, fans started cheering for

ROOKIE catcher Mike Piazza. He slammed a lot of home runs for Los Angeles.

Los Angeles added two power hitters in 2006. Outfielders Andre Ethier and Matt Kemp blasted many homers for the Dodgers. They gave Dodgers fans hope that the team would soon return to the World Series!

MATT KEMP

ANDRE ETHIER

HOW THE DODGERS GOT THEIR NAME

The Dodgers were named while they were playing in Brooklyn, New York. Many trolley cars (vehicles like small trains) ran through the city, and people had to dodge the cars to cross the streets. The team was called the Brooklyn Trolley Dodgers at first. Later, the name was shortened to just Dodgers.

CENTER FIELDER DUKE SNIDER

About the Dodgers

First season: 1884

League/division: National League, West Division

World Series championships:

1955   *4 games to 3 versus New York Yankees*

1959   *4 games to 2 versus Chicago White Sox*

1963   *4 games to 0 versus New York Yankees*

1965   *4 games to 3 versus Minnesota Twins*

1981   *4 games to 2 versus New York Yankees*

1988   *4 games to 1 versus Oakland Athletics*

Dodgers Web site for kids:

http://mlb.mlb.com/la/fan_forum/jrdodgers_form.jsp

Club MLB:

http://web.clubmlb.com/index.html

GLOSSARY

CONTENDERS — teams that have a good chance of winning the championship

PLAYOFFS — all the games (including the World Series) after the regular season that are played to decide who the champion will be

RIVALS — teams that play extra hard against each other

ROOKIE — an athlete playing his or her first year

SCREWBALLS — pitches that make the ball move in a direction the batter does not expect

INDEX